How to Write a

5-Paragraph Essay

Step-by-Step

Step-by-Step Study Skills

Happy Frog Writing Resources
&
PBL Central

Table of Contents

Introduction

Welcome to **How to Write a 5-Paragraph Essay Step-by-Step**.

This workbook teaches you how to write a 5-paragraph essay using a foolproof step-by-step process. Each incremental lesson teaches one step and contains practice examples to build your skill and confidence.

In Part 1, you learn how to plan your essay. You will practice the five steps that take you from the essay prompt – the instructions that your teacher gives you – to an excellent essay outline that is ready to write.

Part 2 teaches you how to write each paragraph in an essay. You will learn exactly what to put in an introductory paragraph, a body paragraph and in the conclusion.

Part 3 provides extra information such as how to title your essay, make a reference/citation list and a brief introduction to editing your essay.

Part 4 contains a handy cheat-sheet that summarizes the steps in planning and writing an essay, as well as worksheets that will help you complete all the steps easily. You can also find a sample essay that demonstrates all the key parts of an essay.

Lastly, Part 5 contains an answer key for the exercises in this workbook.

Get started right now and become an essay expert!

Before you get started....

If you discover you need a bit more support with writing strong paragraphs, we recommend **How to Write an Awesome Paragraph Step-by-Step**, available in print and Kindle on Amazon.

Each incremental lesson in the workbook teaches one step and contains practice examples to build skill and confidence.

Students learn:

- The parts of a paragraph
- How to write a strong topic sentence
- How to write relevant details that connect to the topic sentence
- How to write a meaningful closing sentence

For each step, students learn the basic process and then are taught how to "upgrade" the element to be even stronger. These lessons complement the lessons taught in this book.

You might also benefit from the **How to Plan & Complete School Assignments** workbook.

In this workbook, students learn and practice an easy 4-step process for planning and completing any assignment or project on-time, with no stress.

When You Are Done...

As a next step, check out **How to Edit & Revise Your Essay**. This book teaches you how to effectively and efficiently revise your work so that your essay is clearer, easier to read, and more convincing.

The book includes an extensive editing checklist as well as a detailed reference section explaining each item in the checklist.

Thank You For Your Purchase - Free Editing Checklist

As a thank-you for purchasing this book, you can download a free editing checklist.
https://www.HappyFrogLearning.com/product/editingchecklist

Good luck with your essay writing and editing!

Part 1

Essay Planning

In Part 1, you learn how to plan your essay. Essay planning consists of five steps. You will start with the essay prompt from your teacher and end up with an essay outline, ready to write.

Planning your essay saves you time and results in a better essay. You will also find your essay much easier to write once you have an outline.

Here's an overview of the steps involved. You will learn and practice each step.

Analyze the Essay Prompt

WHAT:

The **essay prompt** is the instruction you get from your teacher about the topic of the essay. For example: *Explain the benefits of playing sports.*

You analyze the essay prompt to make sure you understand what you are required to do.

Analyze Essay Prompt

Make Claim

Identify Supporting Reasons

Claim + Reasons = Essay Thesis

Essay Thesis => Essay Outline

HOW:

Look at the words in the prompt. Look for **topic words** and **direction words**.

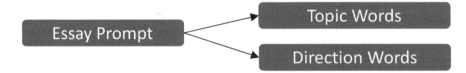

Topic words identify the subject or topic of the essay.

Direction words tell what type of information is expected about the topic. Look for words like 'Explain', 'Compare and contrast', etc. Sometimes essay prompts do not include direction words. In this case, you can assume the prompt means 'Describe' or 'Explain'.

For example: *Explain the benefits of playing sports.*

Topic Words	Direction Words
Benefits of playing sports	Explain the benefits

Practice: Identify Topic Words and Direction Words

Read through these essay prompts and identify the topic words and the direction words. For the last box, add an essay topic that appeals to YOU.

Essay Prompt	Topic Words	Direction Words
Write about someone important to you. Explain why they are important.	*someone important to you*	*Write about Explain why*
What is the biggest challenge facing today's students?		
What are the advantages and disadvantages of school uniforms?		
Compare and contrast two different hobbies.		
Why is it a good idea to graduate high school?		
What makes a good pet?		

Practice: Review Meaning of Direction Words

Some direction words ask for supporting information only. Other direction words ask for information for **and** against a topic, or for similarities **and** differences.

Decide what type of information each of these direction words are asking for. Draw a line between the direction words on the left and the correct interpretation on the right.

Compare and contrast	Describe the negative aspects of...
What are the benefits of...	Describe the good and bad things about...
What are the disadvantages of...	Describe the positive aspects of...
What are the positives and negatives of...	Give reasons why it is important
How important is ...	Describe the similarities and differences

Convert Essay Prompt to a Claim

WHAT:

The next step in writing an essay is to make a claim that is directly related to the essay prompt.

A **claim** is a statement that expresses an opinion or a point of view. It is not a question or an instruction.

For example: Prompt: *Explain the benefits of playing sports.*

Claim: *Sport is very beneficial.*

Analyze Essay Prompt

Make Claim

Identify Supporting Reasons

Claim + Reasons = Essay Thesis

Essay Thesis => Essay Outline

HOW:

Identify the topic words in your essay prompt. Convert the topic words directly to a claim.

Essay prompt with underlined topic words	Claim
What is the best dessert?	Ice-cream is the best dessert.
Describe a time where a disappointment has led to a good outcome.	A disappointment can lead to a good outcome.

Practice: Identify the Claim

For each example, identify which of the three responses is a strong claim. Remember, a claim should answer the essay prompt and be a statement.

For the last example, use an essay prompt that you find interesting.

Essay Prompt	Which is a Strong Claim?
Write about <u>someone important to you</u>. Explain why they are important.	• *My grade 2 teacher is someone who is very important to me.* • ~~*I like my grade 2 teacher.*~~ • ~~*Who should I select as the person most important to me?*~~
What is the biggest challenge facing today's parents?	• Parents should not ban screentime. • Dealing with screentime is the biggest challenge parents face. • Do you want to be a parent?
Should zoos be banned?	• I love visiting the zoo. • Have you ever been to a zoo? • Zoos should not be banned.
What is the right age to get a phone?	• Phones are dangerous for kids. • Children should get phones before they are teenagers. • I am ready for a phone.

Practice: Convert Essay Prompt to a Claim

Read through each essay prompt, underline the topic words and convert them into a claim. A claim is a statement that expresses an opinion or a point of view. It is not a question or an instruction. Make an example of your own in the last box.

Essay Prompt	Claim
Write about <u>someone important to you</u>. Explain why they are important.	*Someone important to me is my grade 2 teacher.*
What are the benefits of learning a musical instrument?	
What are the advantages and disadvantages of a school lunch program?	
Compare and contrast two different sports.	
Why is it a good idea to study hard?	
What makes a good hobby?	
How important is kindness? Explain your answer.	

Identify Supporting Reasons

WHAT:

You now need to find evidence to support your claim. These are the reasons why you believe your claim is true.

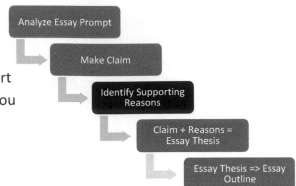

HOW:

1. Look at the **direction words** in your essay prompt. Decide whether you need **one type of reason,** such as the benefits, reasons for, reasons against, **or**,
    whether you need **two types of reasons** such as the pros **&** cons, the advantages **&** disadvantages, etc.

2. Use the table to determine the support your essay requires.

Direction Words ask for one type of information	Direction Words ask for two types of information
Find 3 reasons to support your claim.	Find 2 reasons to support your claim and 1-2 reasons against your claim.

3. The next step is to identify convincing reasons that support your claim. You may be able to think of reasons based on what you already know. If you can't, it's time for some research. Start with a general internet research.

    Need supporting reasons? Search 'WHY your claim'.
    Need non-supporting reasons? Search 'WHY NOT your claim.'

    For example:
    Your claim: *Ice-cream is the best dessert.*
    Search: *Why ice-cream is the best dessert.*

Lastly, make sure your reasons/evidence directly support your claim.

Practice: Check the Reason Supports the Claim

Decide whether each reason directly supports the claim or whether it is not relevant to the claim.

Claim	Reason	Relevant to Claim? Yes/No
Peanut butter sandwiches make the best lunch.	*They are nutritious.*	*Yes*
Peanut butter sandwiches make the best lunch.	Peanuts butter sandwiches became popular during the 1920s.	
The internet has changed our daily life.	We can now access information without going to the library.	
The internet has changed our daily life.	The internet can be slow.	
Climate change is a big problem.	Heat waves are increasing.	
Climate change is a big problem.	Climate change is caused by fossil fuels.	
Fresh fruit is the best dessert.	My favorite fruit is apples.	
Fresh fruit is the best dessert.	Fruit contains many nutrients.	
Schools should start at 7 am.	Students would have lots of free time in the afternoon to do sports.	
Schools should start at 7am.	I live close to my school.	

Practice: Identify Three Reasons

Provide three convincing reasons that support each claim. Use the internet if you need to. In the last box, make up your own claim about something that interests you.

Claim	Reasons
Peanut butter sandwiches make the best lunch.	*1. Nutritious* *2. Easy to make* *3. Quick to eat.*
Schools should have no more than ten students per class.	1. 2. 3.
Teenagers should get paid for doing homework.	1. 2. 3.
You do not need a college degree to be successful.	1. 2. 3.
	1. 2. 3.

Practice: Identify Reasons

Provide two reasons for and two reasons against each claim. Use the internet if you need to.

Claim	Reasons
Peanut butter sandwiches make the best lunch.	*FOR:* *1. Nutritious* *2. Easy to make* *AGAINST:* *1. Bad to eat around people who are allergic to peanuts.* *2. Some peanut butters contain too much sugar.*
Schools should not assign homework.	*FOR:* *1.* *2.* *AGAINST:* *1.* *2.*
All teenagers should get a part-time job.	*FOR:* *1.* *2.* *AGAINST:* *1.* *2.*

Claim + Reasons = Thesis Statement

WHAT:

An **essay thesis statement** is a sentence that ties together the main ideas of your essay. You will use your thesis statement in the introduction of your essay.

An example: *Ice-cream is the best dessert because it is delicious, easy-find and comes in many flavors.*

HOW:

A simple essay thesis consists of a **claim** and three **supporting reasons**. Use this structure when your essay prompt asks only for supporting information.

THESIS = *CLAIM* BECAUSE REASON 1, REASON 2, REASON 3.

Essay prompt: **What is the best dessert?**
Thesis Statement: ***Ice-cream is the best dessert*** because *it is delicious, easy-to-find and has many flavors.*

If your essay prompt asks for 'pros & cons', 'advantages & disadvantages', etc, use a structure like the following.

THESIS =
EVEN THOUGH NEGATIVE REASON, *CLAIM* BECAUSE
POSITIVE REASON 1 AND POSITIVE REASON 2.

Essay prompt: **What are the advantages and disadvantages of ice-cream as a dessert?**
Even though ice-cream must be kept in the freezer, ***it is a great dessert*** because *it is delicious and comes in many flavors.*

Practice: Writing a Thesis Statement

Take each claim and the provided reasons and convert them into a thesis statement.

Claim	Reasons	Thesis statement
Peanut butter sandwiches make the best lunch.	1. *Nutritious* 2. *Easy to make* 3. *Quick to eat*	*Peanut butter sandwiches make the best lunch because they are nutritious, easy to make and quick to eat.*
Getting a part-time job is a good idea for teenagers.	1. Builds your resume 2. Gain work experience 3. Earn money	
The internet has changed our daily life.	1. No longer need printed maps, we can use GPS. 2. Can access information without going to the library. 3. Can connect with friends more easily.	
Cats and dogs are more similar than different.	SIMILARITIES 1. Both are able to survive in the wild. 2. Both have territorial instincts. DIFFERENCE 1. Dogs are more social and cats are more solitary.	

Practice: Analyzing Thesis Statements & Rewriting

Read through each thesis statement and find the problem. Rewrite the thesis statement. In the last row, write your own thesis statement for an essay topic of your choice.

Thesis Statement	Problem	Rewrite
Peanut butter sandwiches make the best lunch.	*Claim but no reasons.*	*Peanut butter sandwiches make the best lunch because they are nutritious, easy to make and quick to eat.*
Going to college is an excellent way to get a good job.		
This paper is about the internet and how bad it is.		
Pollution is a big problem.		
This paper is about good teachers. They are organized, helpful and inspiring.		
School lunchtime should be longer because it's good for kids.		

Essay Prompt to Thesis Statement

WHAT:

You are now ready to go all the way from essay prompt to thesis statement. Remember, a thesis statement has a claim and 3-4 reasons. The reasons may all support the claim, or some might provide an alternate viewpoint.

For example: Prompt: *Explain the benefits and disadvantages of playing sports.*
Thesis statement:

Although sport can cause injury, sport is very beneficial because it is good for your body, good for your mind and helps you be social.

HOW:

Follow the steps you have learned.
1. Examine the essay prompt. Look for **topic** words and **direction words**.
2. Convert the **topic words** into a **claim**.
3. Examine the **direction words** and determine the type of reasons you need. Research/Brainstorm your **reasons**.
4. Put the claim and the reasons together into a **thesis statement**.

Essay Prompt	Thesis statement
What is the best dessert?	Ice-cream is the best dessert because it is delicious, easy-to-find and has many flavors.
Describe a person you look up to.	I look up to my grade 2 teacher because she was kind, helpful and understood my challenges.

Practice: Convert an Essay Prompt to a Thesis Statement

Read through each essay prompt and create a thesis statement.
- Identify the topic words and the direction words.
- Convert the topic words into a claim.
- Identify your reasons.
- Finally, convert your claim and reasons into a thesis statement.

Essay Prompt:	Claim:
Should <u>children be allowed to access the internet</u>?	*Children should be allowed to access the internet.*
Reasons: *1. Educational* *2. Fun* *3. Something families can do together*	**Thesis Statement:** *Children should be allowed to access the internet because the internet is educational, fun, and there are many online games families can play together.*

Essay Prompt:	Claim:
What is your favorite movie? Explain why.	
Reasons:	**Thesis Statement:**

Practice: Convert an Essay Prompt to a Thesis Statement

Convert each essay prompt into a thesis statement.

Essay Prompt: Does class size matter?	Claim:
Reasons:	Thesis Statement:

Essay Prompt: What are the advantages and disadvantages of a college education?	Claim:
Reasons:	Thesis Statement:

Practice: Convert an Essay Prompt to a Thesis Statement

Convert the essay prompt into a thesis statement. In the last box, use an essay prompt of your choosing.

Essay Prompt:	Claim:
What are the pros and cons of social media?	
Reasons:	**Thesis Statement:**

Essay Prompt:	Claim:
Reasons:	**Thesis Statement:**

Thesis Statement to Essay Outline

WHAT:

An essay outline is a short summary of what you plan to write in each of the three parts of your essay: the introduction, the body paragraphs and the conclusion.

Analyze Essay Prompt

Make Claim

Identify Supporting Reasons

Claim + Reasons = Essay Thesis

Essay Thesis => Essay Outline

HOW:

Once you have an essay thesis, it is easy to create your essay outline.

Use an essay outline like the one below and place the parts of your thesis statement in the relevant sections.

Introduction   **Thesis Statement (= claim + 3 reasons)**

Body Paragraph 1

    Write about Positive Reason 1 and how it supports your claim.

Body Paragraph 2

    Write about Positive Reason 2 and how it supports your claim.

Body Paragraph 3

    Write about Positive Reason 3 and how it supports your claim. OR, write about Negative Reason 1 and why it isn't a big problem.

Conclusion   **Reword Thesis Statement**

Practice: Convert Thesis Statement to Essay Outline

Convert each thesis statement to an essay outline.

Thesis: Zoos should be banned because animals need space, they can get sick from other animals and they can get lonely.

Introduction: Zoos should be banned because animals need space, they can get sick from other animals and they can get lonely.

Body Paragraph 1: Write about why animals need space and why that means zoos should be banned.

Body Paragraph 2: Write about how animals can get sick from other animals and why that means zoos should be banned.

Body Paragraph 3: Write about how animals can get lonely and why that means zoos should be banned.

Conclusion: Zoos cannot provide animals with a safe environment that gives them space and keeps them physically and mentally healthy. Therefore, zoos should be banned.

Thesis: School uniforms are a good choice because they are inexpensive, make it easier to get ready for school and promote a sense of community.

Introduction

Body Paragraph 1

Body Paragraph 2

Body Paragraph 3

Conclusion

Practice: Convert Thesis Statement to Essay Outline

Convert each thesis statement to an essay outline.

Thesis: Homework should be banned because it takes too much time, cuts into family time and doesn't increase grades.

Introduction

Body Paragraph 1

Body Paragraph 2

Body Paragraph 3

Conclusion

Thesis: Even though smaller classes are expensive, smaller classes are better because students can get more help and form a closer bond with their fellow students.

Introduction

Body Paragraph 1

Body Paragraph 2

Body Paragraph 3

Conclusion

Practice: Convert Thesis Statement to Essay Outline

Convert each thesis statement to an essay Outline.

Thesis: Students should not be allowed to bring phones to class because they distract the student from learning, distract other students and can also distract the teacher.

Introduction

Body Paragraph 1

Body Paragraph 2

Body Paragraph 3

Conclusion

Thesis: Students should be allowed to bring phones to class because they can access information quickly, set reminders for homework and access educational apps.

Introduction

Body Paragraph 1

Body Paragraph 2

Body Paragraph 3

Conclusion

Essay Prompt to Essay Outline

WHAT:

You now know how to convert an essay prompt into an outline for an awesome essay.

HOW:

Follow the steps you have learned. These steps are summarized below.

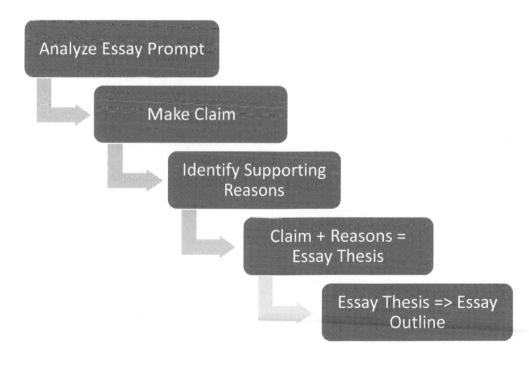

Practice: Convert Essay Prompt to Essay Outline

Convert the essay prompt to an essay outline.

Essay Prompt: Should students be allowed to wear makeup to school?

Claim:

Three Reasons:

Thesis Statement:

Outline:

Introduction

Body Paragraph 1

Body Paragraph 2

Body Paragraph 3

Conclusion

Practice: Convert Essay Prompt to Essay Outline

Convert the essay prompt to an essay outline.

Essay Prompt: What are the pros and cons of teachers using games to teach?

Claim:

Three Reasons:

Thesis Statement:

Outline:

Introduction

Body Paragraph 1

Body Paragraph 2

Body Paragraph 3

Conclusion

Practice: Convert Essay Prompt to Essay Outline

Choose your own essay prompt and convert it into an essay outline.

Essay Prompt:

Claim:

Three Reasons:

Thesis Statement:

Outline:

Introduction

Body Paragraph 1

Body Paragraph 2

Body Paragraph 3

Conclusion

Part 2

Writing the Essay

You now have a good understanding of how to convert an essay prompt into an essay outline. In this section, you will learn how to write each of the paragraphs in your essay.

An essay has three types of paragraphs:

- Introductory or First Paragraph
- Body Paragraphs
- Conclusion or Final Paragraph

Introduction
Body Paragraph 1
Body Paragraph 2
Body Paragraph 3
Conclusion

In Part 2, you will learn how to write each of these types of paragraphs.

Writing the Introductory Paragraph

WHAT:

The introductory paragraph is the first paragraph in your essay. This paragraph lets the reader know what the essay is about and what they can expect to read in the essay.

Introduction
Body Paragraph 1
Body Paragraph 2
Body Paragraph 3
Conclusion

HOW:

The introductory paragraph consists of three parts: the hook, the transition to the thesis statement, and the thesis statement.

We will teach you how to write each of these sections (except for the thesis statement, which you have already written!)

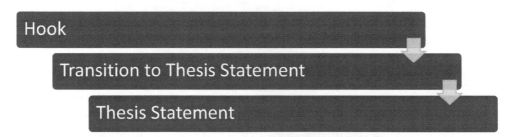

Hook

Transition to Thesis Statement

Thesis Statement

Introductory Paragraph	Example
Hook	39% of Americans eat dessert at least once per week.
Transition to Thesis	Although there are many choices for dessert,
Thesis Statement	Ice-cream is the best dessert because it is delicious, easy-to-find and comes in many flavors.

Practice: Identify Introductory Paragraph Components

Identify each part of the introductory paragraphs.

1. Hook	Sweet desserts have been around since the middle ages. These days there are many desserts to choose from. However, ice-cream is the best dessert because it is delicious, easy-find and comes in many flavors.
2. Transition to Thesis	
3. Thesis Statement	

1. Hook	There are more than 2 billion websites on the internet. While not all of these websites are good, children should be allowed to access the internet because the internet is educational, fun, and there are many online games that families can play together.
2. Transition to Thesis	
3. Thesis Statement	

1. Hook	Children often ask for internet access. However, not everything children want is good for them. Children should not be allowed to access the internet because staring at a screen is unhealthy, there are dangerous places on the internet and their time is better spent playing with friends.
2. Transition to Thesis	
3. Thesis Statement	

1. Hook	Only 20% of US schools start their day at 7:45 or earlier. Many school are wasting part of the day. School should start at 7am because it allows plenty of time to play in the afternoon, time for an afternoon job and lots of time to do homework.
2. Transition to Thesis	
3. Thesis Statement	

Intro Paragraph - Writing the Hook

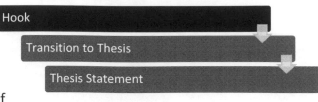

WHAT:

The hook is the very first sentence of your essay.

The purpose of the hook is to grab your reader's attention.

HOW:

Here are some suggestions for creating an interesting hook.

- **Ask a question** that's relevant to your thesis statement. Make sure it's not a question that everyone knows the answer to. The question should make the reader start to think.

- **Include an interesting fact**.

- **Include a relevant quotation**. The quotation must relate to your essay topic.

- **Begin with a compelling or unexpected statement**. Again, it must be related to your claim or thesis statement.

There is no single 'correct' hook. So, brainstorm/research a few and choose the one you prefer best. Try:

- 'fun facts about YOUR ESSAY TOPIC' or
- 'interesting facts about YOUR ESSAY TOPIC'

If that doesn't reveal some interesting facts, try searches with WHERE, WHY, HOW MANY, WHEN, WHAT, WHY + YOUR ESSAY TOPIC.

On the next page, you can find some sample hooks for different essay topics.

Intro Paragraph - Writing the Hook Continued

	Potential Hooks
Essay Topic: Should children be allowed to access the internet?	There are more than 2 billion websites on the internet.
	4 billion out of the 7 billion people on earth are already on the internet.
	66% of US children have internet access at home.
Thesis Statement for an essay about the novel *Hatchet*: Brian's wilderness experience turns him from a child into a young man.	Could you survive alone in the wilderness?
	According to a study by the Transportation Safety Board of Canada, only about 10% of occupants escape from float planes that crash in water. Brian Robeson, in Gary Paulsen's novel *Hatchet*, was extremely lucky.
	It took only 54 days to change Brian from a child into a young man.

In contrast, the following hooks don't quite work for the *Hatchet* essay thesis statement.

- He was alone. In a roaring plane with no pilot he was alone. Alone. *Hatchet*, Chapter 1.

  This is a dramatic hook, but it does not really relate to the claim of new-found maturity or wilderness survival. It would be a good hook for a different claim.

- Did you know it is difficult to light a fire without matches or a lighter?

The problem with this hook is that it asks a question that everyone knows the answer to. It does not make a good hook.

Practice: Writing Hooks

Write three potential hooks for each essay prompt. For the last box, use a topic that you find interesting.

Essay Topic	Potential Hooks
What are the advantages and disadvantages of school uniforms?	

Essay Topic	Potential Hooks
Why is it a good idea to graduate high school?	

Essay Topic	Potential Hooks

Intro Paragraph - Writing the Transition

Hook

Transition to Thesis

Thesis Statement

WHAT:

The transition sentence connects your hook to your thesis statement.

HOW:

Write out your hook and your thesis statement. Think of a sentence (or part of a sentence) that connects to both the hook and the thesis statement. The goal is to transition from the hook to your claim.

There is no single 'correct' transition. Experiment until the transition is smooth.

Here are some examples:

Hook	There are more than 2 billion websites on the internet.
Transition	Even though not all these sites are high-quality,
Thesis Statement	Children should be allowed to access the internet because the internet is educational, fun, and there are many online games families can play together.

Hook	66% of US children have internet access at home.
Transition	Although many parents worry about screen-time,
Thesis Statement	Children should be allowed to access the internet because the internet is educational, fun, and there are many online games families can play together.

Practice: Writing Transition Statements

Write a transition statement for each example.

Hook	October 14 is National Dessert Day.
Transition	
Thesis Statement	Fresh fruit is the best dessert because it is nutritious, delicious and easy to prepare.

Hook	The first known use of the word 'dessert' was in the 1600s.
Transition	
Thesis Statement	Fresh fruit is the best dessert because it is nutritious, delicious and easy to prepare.

Hook	The US National School Lunch program costs more than 13 billion dollars per year.
Transition	
Thesis Statement	Schools should include a free lunch because it helps students learn, helps poorer students and reduces childhood obesity.

Writing the Intro Paragraph - Final

WHAT:

You are now ready to write an introductory paragraph for any essay.

Introduction
Body Paragraph 1
Body Paragraph 2
Body Paragraph 3
Conclusion

HOW:

Remember, your introductory paragraph consists of:

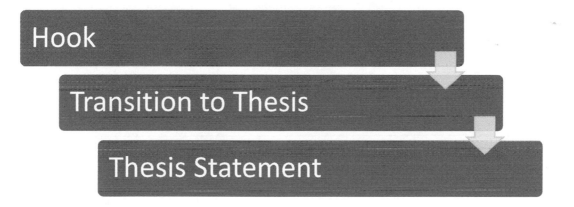

Hook

Transition to Thesis

Thesis Statement

Don't forget:

Start with creating a strong thesis statement. Next, find a compelling hook. Lastly, link the two with a transition phrase or sentence.

Practice: Write Introductory Paragraphs

Write an introductory paragraph to suit each thesis statement.

Essay Topic: Should students be allowed to bring phones to class?

Hook:_____

_____

Transition: _____

_____

Thesis Statement: Students should not be allowed to bring phones to class because they distract the student from learning, distract other students and can also distract the teacher.

Essay Topic: Should students be allowed to bring phones to class?

Hook:_____

_____

Transition: _____

_____

Thesis Statement: Students should be allowed to bring phones to class because they can access information quickly, set reminders for homework and access educational apps.

Practice: Write Introductory Paragraphs

Write an introductory paragraph to suit each thesis statement.

Essay Topic: Should teens be allowed to drink coffee?

Hook:_____

_____

Transition: _____

_____

Thesis Statement: Teens should be allowed to drink coffee because caffeine can lower a person's risk for heart disease, increase alertness and focus, and coffee contains some healthy antioxidants.

Essay Topic: Should teens be allowed to drink coffee?

Hook:_____

_____

Transition: _____

_____

Thesis Statement: Teens should not be allowed to drink coffee because caffeine can cause the body to lose calcium, can bring on a jittery feeling, and can cause insomnia.

Body Paragraph - Overview

Introduction
Body Paragraph 1
Body Paragraph 2
Body Paragraph 3
Conclusion

WHAT:

Body paragraphs are the main part of an essay. They come after the introduction paragraph.

For most essays, each body paragraph provides evidence why your essay claim is true. These are **SUPPORTING** paragraphs.

If you are writing a 'compare & contrast', or 'advantages & disadvantages' essay, some of your body paragraphs may contain reasons against your claim. These are **NON-SUPPORTING PARAGRAPHS** or **COUNTERARGUMENTS**.

In the next pages, you will learn step-by-step how to write these two types of paragraphs.

Body Paragraph - Supporting

WHAT:

A supporting body paragraph provides evidence why your essay claim is true.

HOW:

A supporting body paragraph consists of:

Topic Sentence

Evidence

Connection to Claim

Here is an example of a supporting body paragraph with these sections identified.

Essay Claim: Zoos should be banned.

1. Topic Sentence	[[**1** Zoos cannot provide the same space that animals have in the wild.]] [[**2** According to a Guardian article from 2003, tigers and lions have around 18,000 times less space in zoos than they would in the wild.]] [[**3** Zoos should be banned because they do not provide enough space for animals.]]
2. Evidence/Support	
3. Connection to Essay Claim	

Next you will practice identifying these parts of the body paragraph. After that, you will learn how to write each part to create a strong paragraph that supports your claim.

Practice: Identify Supporting Paragraph Components

Identify each part of the supporting paragraph.

Essay Thesis: Teens should be allowed to drink coffee because caffeine can lower a person's risk for heart disease, increase alertness and focus, and coffee contains some healthy antioxidants.

1. Topic Sentence	Caffeine can lower your risk of heart disease. According to researchers from the University of Colorado, a cup of coffee can lower your risk of heart disease by 5%. Teenagers should be allowed to drink coffee so they can lower their risk of heart disease.
2. Evidence/Support	
3. Connection to Essay Claim	

Essay Thesis: Children should be allowed to access the internet because the internet is educational, fun, and there are many online games families can play together.

Topic Sentence	Children should be allowed to access the internet because it is very educational. You can find videos that explain school subjects such as English or science. You can play online games to practice math. Children need internet access to benefit from these educational resources.
Evidence/Support	
Connection to Essay Claim	

Body Paragraph – Topic Sentence

Now let's learn how to write each part of the paragraph, starting with the topic sentence.

Topic Sentence

Evidence

Connection to Claim

WHAT:

The **topic sentence** is the first sentence in a body paragraph. The topic sentence states the main claim that you are making in this paragraph.

HOW:

1. Look back at your outline. Review your essay claim and the reason listed for this paragraph.
2. Make a statement that expresses the reason.

For example:

Essay Claim: Zoos should be banned
Reason: Not enough space for the animals.

Possible Topic Sentences:

- Zoos should be banned because they do not have enough space for animals.
- Zoos do not have enough space for animals.
- The lack of space for animals is an excellent reason for banning zoos.
- Animals need space to thrive.

Practice: Writing a Topic Sentence

Write a topic sentence for each example.

Essay Thesis:	
Children should be allowed to access the internet because the internet is educational, fun, and there are many online games families can play together.	
Claim:	**Reason # 3:**
Possible Topic Sentence:	

Essay Thesis:	
Students should be allowed to bring phones to class because they can access information quickly, set reminders for homework and access educational apps.	
Claim:	**Reason # 3:**
Possible Topic Sentence:	

Practice: Writing a Topic Sentence

Write a topic sentence for each example. For the last one, use a thesis statement of your choice.

Essay Thesis:	
Teens should be allowed to drink coffee because caffeine can lower a person's risk for heart disease, increase alertness and focus, and coffee contains some healthy antioxidants.	
Claim:	**Reason # 2:**
Possible Topic Sentence:	

Essay Thesis:	
Claim:	**Reason # 2:**
Possible Topic Sentence:	

Body Paragraph – Providing Evidence

WHAT:

After the topic sentence, you write 1-3 sentences providing evidence for the claim you made in the topic sentence.

| Topic Sentence |
| Evidence |
| Connection to Claim |

HOW:

1. Review your topic sentence.
2. If necessary, do some research to find evidence to support your claim.
3. Write the sentences to support your claim.

For example:

Topic Sentence: Children should have access to the internet so they can benefit from educational apps.

Possible Evidence for this Topic Sentence:
- Educational apps offer an active form of learning that suits many children.
- With apps, children can learn at any time and don't need to wait for a teacher.
- With educational apps, children can get extra practice in areas they are weak.

Topic Sentence + Evidence Sentences:
Children should have access to the internet so they can benefit from educational apps. Educational apps offer an active form of learning that suits many children. Also, children can learn at any time and don't need to wait for a teacher. In addition, with educational apps, children can get extra practice in areas they are weak.

Practice: Adding Evidence

Write some evidence sentences for each topic sentence.

Topic Sentence: Learning a second language benefits your brain.
Evidence Brainstorm/Research:
Evidence Sentence(s):

Topic Sentence: Caffeine can have health benefits.
Evidence Brainstorm/Research:
Evidence Sentence(s):

Practice: Adding Evidence

Write some evidence sentences for each topic sentence. In the last table, use a topic sentence for a topic that interests you.

Topic Sentence:
Smoking is bad for your health.
Evidence Brainstorm/Research:
Evidence Sentence(s):

Topic Sentence:
Evidence Brainstorm/Research:
Evidence Sentence(s):

Body Paragraph – Linking Back to Essay Claim

| Topic Sentence |
| Evidence |
| Connection to Claim |

WHAT:

The last step in a body paragraph is to connect your evidence back to the original essay claim.

HOW:

1. Review your essay claim.
2. Write a sentence that links the evidence you provided back to the essay claim.

For example:

Essay Claim: Children should have access to the internet.
Reason: They can access educational apps.

Evidence Sentences	Connecting to Essay Claim
With educational apps, children can get extra practice in areas they are weak. They can also move ahead in areas they are strong.	Children should have access to the internet so they can get these educational benefits.

Practice: Connecting to Essay Claim

Write a final sentence for each paragraph that connects the paragraph back to the essay claim.

Essay Claim: Schools should have uniforms.

Topic Sentence: School uniforms instill a sense of equality.

Evidence Sentences:

When students wear a school uniform, competitive feelings about looks are reduced. Students can stand out because of their character and not their clothes.

Connection to Claim Sentence:

Essay Claim: Public transit should be free.

Topic Sentence: Free public transport would reduce the number of cars on the road.

Evidence Sentences:

Global warming is a serious issue and if public transport was free, more people would use it, taking cars off the road. One train could take 2000 cars off the road.

Connection to Claim Sentence:

Body Paragraph – Non-Supporting

WHAT:

A non-supporting body paragraph provides evidence against your essay claim. Often additional evidence is provided that counters this non-supporting evidence.

HOW:

A non-supporting body paragraph consists of:

- Topic Sentence
- Evidence
- Counter-Evidence
- Connection to Claim

Since you already know how to write most of these sections, you only need to learn about writing the counter-evidence section.

Here is an example of a non-supporting body paragraph for an essay with a claim of 'Zoos should be banned.'

1. Topic Sentence	[[**1** Some people argue that zoos should not be banned because they help endangered animals.]] [[**2** Many zoos are part of the Species Survival Plan which has helped bring black-footed ferrets, California condors and several other endangered species back from the brink of extinction]] [[**3** However, you do not have to be a zoo to participate in the Species Survival Plan and many zoos do not participate.]] [[**4** Hence, helping endangered animals is not a convincing reason to allow zoos.]].
2. Evidence/Support	
3. Counter-Evidence.	
4. Connection to Essay Claim	

Practice: Identify Non-Supporting Paragraph Parts

Identify each part of the non-supporting paragraph.

Essay Thesis: Even though caffeine can cause insomnia, teens should be allowed to drink coffee because caffeine can increase alertness and focus and coffee contains some healthy antioxidants.

1. Topic Sentence	Coffee does have some negative affects. Specifically, caffeine can cause insomnia because it is a stimulant. However, this problem is easily avoided by only drinking coffee before 3pm. Therefore, the potential for insomnia should not prevent teens from drinking coffee.
2. Evidence/Support	
3. Counter-evidence	
4. Connection to Essay Claim	

Essay Thesis: Even though the internet has some dangerous places, children should be allowed to access the internet because the internet is educational, fun, and there are many online games families can play together.

1. Topic Sentence	The internet has many dangerous places. The news often contains articles about some of the problem areas and dangers. However, the real world has dangers, too. Rather than banning children from the internet, we should be teaching them how to be safe in all the worlds they inhabit. The dangers of the internet are no reason to ban children from the internet.
2. Evidence/Support	
3. Counter-evidence	
4. Connection to Essay Claim	

Body Paragraph – Counter-Evidence

WHAT:

The counter-evidence section argues against the non-supporting evidence you just provided.

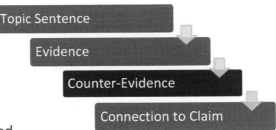

HOW:

Provide a reason why the evidence you provided is not really an argument against your claim.

Your research should provide you with information to counter the counterargument. Usually, arguments are rebutted in one of four ways:

- Accept the reasoning but **minimize its important** or significance.

- **Reject the claim** made in the counterargument by using evidence/reasoning.

- **Reject the evidence** provided by using evidence/reasoning.

- **Reject the reasoning** in how this claim counters your essay claim.

You can signal your opposing information with transition phrases such as.

- Even though …
- Despite …
- However, …
- Nevertheless, …

See the next page for an example.

Body Paragraph – Counter-Evidence

For example:

Essay Claim: Coffee is good for your health

Topic Sentence in a non-supporting paragraph	There is evidence that coffee can be bad for you.
Evidence supporting topic sentence	For example, more than four cups a day can lead to an early death.
Counter-evidence	However, anything in excess can be bad for you. There is much research to show that a reasonable intake of coffee has health benefits.
Link back to original claim	Therefore for most people who drink just a few cups per day, we can still say that coffee is good for your health.

Practice: Providing Counter-Evidence

Write a counter-evidence sentence for each paragraph that supports your original claim.

Essay Claim: Schools should have uniforms.
Topic Sentence in non-supporting paragraph: Buying school uniforms is an added expense for families.
Evidence supporting topic sentence: School uniforms can cost about $200 per outfit. And families still have to buy everyday clothes as well.
Counter-evidence sentence:

Essay Claim: Public transit should be free.
Topic Sentence in non-supporting paragraph: Providing free transit would be extremely expensive.
Evidence supporting topic sentence: The city would need to buy more buses and pay more drivers.
Counter-evidence sentence:

Writing a Body Paragraph – Transition Phrases

WHAT:

Transition phrases are phrases that give signposts to a reader about what is coming next. They are used frequently in the body and concluding paragraphs in an essay to make it easier to understand.

For example, saying "first," lets your reader know you will be giving several pieces of information, or will be telling them several steps. When you say "second" or "next", you let your reader know they are getting the second piece of information.

Another example is the transition word "however." This lets the reader know that you may be about to say something opposite to what they might expect.

For example: I like ice cream. However, pie is my favorite dessert.

HOW:

On the next page you will find a table of common transitions. The following exercise pages will give you practice in using them.

List of Common Transition Words

Beginning	First, To begin with, In the beginning, One example
Continue	Next, Also, After that, To continue, In addition, Furthermore, Another reason, Another example, Eventually
Alike	Similarly, Along the same lines, In comparison, Additionally, Likewise
Different	However, Although, On the other hand, In contrast
Result	As a result, Consequently, For these reasons, Therefore
Time	Suddenly, Occasionally, Frequently, When, Until
Example	For example, For instance, To illustrate
Quote	As X says, According to X, X states
Finish	In conclusion, In summary, Last, Finally, In the end, To sum up, In short
Supporting Paragraph Transitions	First, Next, Another reason, On the one hand
Counterargument Transitions	However, However, it can also be argued that, In contrast, On the other hand, In opposition to

Practice: Find the Transition Words

Underline all the transitions in these paragraphs.

There are over 100 buildings in the world more than one thousand feet tall. However, the tallest building is the Burj Khalifa. The Burj Khalifa is amazing for several reasons.

First, this building is 2,722 feet tall, almost 1 kilometer! Can you imagine how tall that is?

Second, the Burj Khalifa cost $1.5 billion dollars to build. Construction of the Burj Khalifa started in 2004 and finished in 2009.

The Burj Khalifa building is in Dubai. Although most people think Dubai is a country, it is not. In fact, it is one of the seven Emirates in the United Arab Emirates.

Even the name of the building is interesting. Burj means tower in Arabic. Khalifa is the name of the leader of the United Arab Emirates.

The Burj Khalifa has won many awards. It has broken records for the highest restaurant and the highest swimming pool. In addition, it has the highest observation deck in the world.

To sum up, the Burj Khalifa is truly amazing!

Practice: Choose the Transition 1

Choose the correct transition from the choices available.

_____ the weather was bad, Jenny took an umbrella with her.

1. Because

2. In addition

3. Only

_____ , these are the reasons why we should have a longer lunch break.

1. Because

2. In conclusion

3. Frequently

Tamra likes art. _____ , her favorite subject is math.

1. First

2. Although

3. However

I cleaned the kitchen, did my homework and tidied my room. _____ , I should be allowed to go play with my friends.

1. Only

2. As a result

3. However

Practice: Writing Transitions 1

Practice using the transitions by making up a sentence to go with each of the listed transitions.

For example, _____

_____

In addition, _____

_____

To begin with, _____

_____

In conclusion, _____

_____

However, _____

_____

Practice: Writing Transitions 2

Practice using the transitions by making up a sentence to go with each of the listed transitions.

Next, _____

_____

Similarly, _____

_____

Although, _____

_____

As mom says, _____

_____

Frequently, _____

_____

Writing a Body Paragraph - Final

WHAT:

You now know how to to write supporting and non-supporting body paragraph from an outline.

HOW:

A supporting body paragraph consists of:

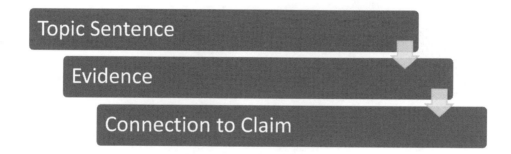

A non-supporting body paragraph consists of:

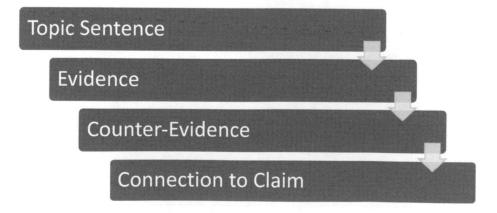

Let's practice writing body paragraphs.

Practice: Write Body Paragraphs

Choose one of the reasons in the thesis statement and write a body paragraph to support that reason.

Thesis Statement: Students should not be allowed to bring phones to class because they distract the student from learning, distract other students and can also distract the teacher.

Reason I choose to write about:_____

Topic Sentence: _____
_____

Evidence Brainstorming/Research:

Evidence Sentences: _____
_____
_____
_____

Link to Essay Claim: _____
_____

Practice: Write Body Paragraphs

Choose one of the reasons in the thesis statement and write a body paragraph to support that reason. Feel free to write the counterargument if you wish. For even more practice, write all three body paragraphs and the counterargument paragraph.

Thesis Statement: Although teenagers think smoking is cool, smoking should be banned because it is addictive, bad for your health and costs a lot.

Reason I choose to write about:_____

Topic Sentence: _____

_____

Evidence Brainstorming/Research:

Evidence/Counter-Evidence Sentences: _____

_____

_____

_____

Link to Essay Claim: _____

_____

Writing the Conclusion - Overview

WHAT:

The concluding paragraph is the final paragraph in your essay.

| Introduction |
| Body Paragraph 1 |
| Body Paragraph 2 |
| Body Paragraph 3 |
| **Conclusion** |

HOW:

A concluding paragraph consists of these sections:

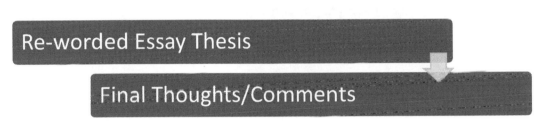

Re-worded Essay Thesis

Final Thoughts/Comments

Typically, a transition like 'in conclusion' is also added. For example:

Original Thesis: Smoking should be banned because it is addictive, bad for your health and costs a lot.

1. Restatement of Thesis	[[**1** In conclusion, even if smoking doesn't kill you or ruin your health, it should still be banned because it is addictive and wastes your money.]] [[**2** 480,000 people die in the US every year from smoking. Let's change that.]]
2. Final Thoughts	

The next lessons will teach you how to reword your thesis and add final thoughts.

Writing the Conclusion - Reword Thesis

Re-worded Essay Thesis

Final Thoughts/Comments

WHAT:

Reword your thesis statement to start bringing your essay to a close.

HOW:

Say the same thing as your original thesis statement but change the wording. Use more than one sentence if you need to.

Practice: Reword Thesis

Original Thesis	Reworded Thesis
Students should not be allowed to bring phones to class because they distract the student from learning, distract other students and can also distract the teacher.	
Fresh fruit is the best dessert because it is nutritious, delicious and easy to prepare.	

Writing the Conclusion - Final Thoughts

Re-worded Essay Thesis

Final Thoughts/Comments

WHAT:

The final thoughts sentence brings your essay to a close.

HOW:

There are several ways to add a final thought to your essay.

- Add a Future Thought
- Add Encouragement to Action
- Add a Question about the Content
- Add a Personal Opinion

Here are some examples how each of these strategies could be used in a sample paragraph.

In conclusion, children should be allowed to access the many benefits of the internet. As we have seen, the internet is fun, educational and families can play together. While it can be dangerous, this danger is easily handled.

- If we want our children to be good future citizens, we should not exclude them from our greatest information resource.

- Let's make sure all children have appropriate access to the wonderful benefits that the internet can provide.

- Is it really a good idea to limit such a wonderful resource when it can provide so much benefit?

- In summary, the internet should be available to children as long as it is limited appropriately.

Practice: Adding Final Thoughts

Write final thought sentences for each example. Try to use a different strategy for each example.

Essay Thesis:
Teens should be allowed to drink coffee because caffeine can lower a person's risk for heart disease, increase alertness and focus, and coffee contains some healthy antioxidants.
Final Thoughts:

Essay Thesis:
Students should learn a second language in school because it increases their employment potential, benefits their brain, and gives students an understanding of other cultures.
Final Thoughts:

Essay Thesis:
Although there are many delicious desserts, fresh fruit is the best dessert because it is nutritious, delicious and easy to prepare.
Final Thoughts:

Part 3

Final Touches

Congratulations, you now know the basics for writing an excellent essay.

In this section, we cover some final components to help you write your best essay ever. You will learn about:

- Essay titles
- Citing your references
- Editing & revising

Writing the Essay Title

WHAT:

The title is the heading at the top of your essay.

The purpose of the title is to let the reader know what the essay will be about.

HOW:

To come up with a good title, consider using a reworded version of:

- Your essay claim

- The essay question from the teacher

For example, if your essay prompt is:

- Discuss the effects of technology on war.

Your title could be:

- The Effects of Technology on War

If your essay claim is:

- Cats are better than dogs.

Your title could be:

- Cats vs Dogs. Which is better?

- Cats are Better than Dogs

Practice: Writing Titles

Write three possible titles for each essay prompt.

Essay Prompt	Possible Titles
Should students be allowed to use phones in class?	
What is the best breakfast?	
Should zoos be banned?	
What challenges do today's teenagers face that are different from the challenges their parents faced?	
Compare and contrast two novels set in your state or city.	

Including References/Citations

WHAT:

A reference list is a list at the end of your essay that records all the books, articles, or internet resources whose information you mention in your essay.

The purpose of the reference list is to let the reader know where your information came from. Readers can check your references to learn more about what you said.

WHEN:

Whenever you used evidence or data in your essay, you should include the source of that evidence in your reference list.   Places where you might have cited evidence or data include:

- Introductory paragraph: Essay hook

- Body paragraph: Evidence sentences.

- Conclusion: Final thoughts

HOW:

References appear in two places in your essay.   They appear in the body of the essay when you mention the data/evidence. They also appear at the end of the essay in a reference list.

On the next page, you will learn how to do each type of reference/citation.

Including References/Citations

HOW: In-Essay References

When you mention data/evidence that you got from somewhere else, you need to tell the reader where you got that information. You can add this information in various ways.

- By mentioning it in the sentence.

  According to the Center for Disease Control and Prevention, 480,000 Americans die from cigarette smoking each year.

- By adding a citation at the end of the sentence showing the source and the year the content was published.

  480,000 Americans die from cigarette smoking each year (CDC 2023).

  The source is typically either the author surname or the website name abbreviated.

HOW: Reference List

Every information source listed in your essay should also be listed in the reference list at the end of your essay. This list gives the actual details for how to find that resource.

Reference lists can be formatted in different ways, depending on what **style guide** your teacher prefers (E.g. MLA, APA, or Chicago styles).

If your teacher has not introduced a style guide, use a consistent format like the following. All entries should be ordered alphabetically by the first letter.

Including References/Citations

HOW: Reference List Continued

General Format for Books
Author-Last-Name, Author-First-Name. "Title". Publisher, Year.

Matthews, Jay. "How to Write an Awesome Paragraph Step-by-Step." Happy Frog Press, 2020.

General Format for Web Resource
Author-Last-Name, Author-First-Name. "Title of Article/Page/Video". Title of Website, Year. Website URL.

Note: if a web resource does not have an author, start with the page title.

"Citation Styles & Tools." Washington University Libraries, 2020. https://guides.lib.uw.edu/c.php?g=341448&p=4076094

Practice: References/Citation

Choose 8 books, websites, or videos and convert them into the proper format for a reference list. Don't forget to arrange them alphabetically.

Editing Your Essay

WHAT:

Once you have finished your first draft, it is important to allow time to edit and revise your essay. A quick edit can be the difference between an average grade and an excellent one.

HOW:

As a first step, download our free editing checklist.
https://www.HappyFrogLearning.com/product/editingchecklist

Essay revision consists of three main steps.

1. First you check to ensure that all of the required **structural** components of the essay are present. This ensures you have a strong essay structure that is easily understood.

    Structural components include: hook, thesis statement, introductory, body and conclusion paragraphs, etc.

2. Once your essay structure has been strengthened, you revise to **improve the style**.

    This involves choosing strong over weak words, making sure you include transitions phrases, etc.

3. Finally, your last check focuses on **mechanics** like spelling and grammar.

The editing checklist will step you through each of these stages.

Editing Your Essay continued

Editing is an important skill for all students and for all subjects. Once you have mastered the essay skills developed in this book, we recommend working through the companion book, **How to Edit and Revise Your Essay**.

This book teaches you how to effectively and efficiently revise your work so that your essay is clearer, easier to read, and more convincing.

The book includes an extensive editing checklist as well as a detailed reference section explaining each item in the checklist.

Part 4

Essay Cheat-Sheet, Planning Worksheets & Sample Essay

Congratulations, you have finished the learning part of the workbook.

In this section, you will find a handy cheat-sheet to use as a reference when writing your essays. Use this helpful one-pager to remind yourself of the key steps in planning and writing an essay.

You'll also find some essay planning & writing worksheets, which are designed to help you remember the steps in planning and writing an essay. We recommend you use these pages to plan and write your essays until the steps become automatic.

Lastly, in this section, you will also find a sample essay. You can study this to see all the components you have learned in this workbook in action in an actual essay.

Essay Planning & Writing Cheat Sheet

Planning

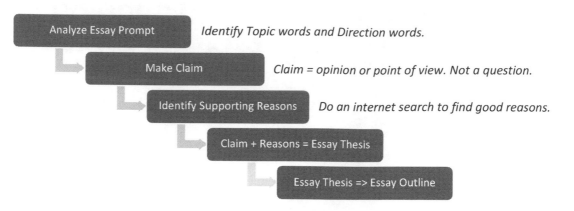

Analyze Essay Prompt — *Identify Topic words and Direction words.*

Make Claim — *Claim = opinion or point of view. Not a question.*

Identify Supporting Reasons — *Do an internet search to find good reasons.*

Claim + Reasons = Essay Thesis

Essay Thesis => Essay Outline

Writing

Introductory Paragraph

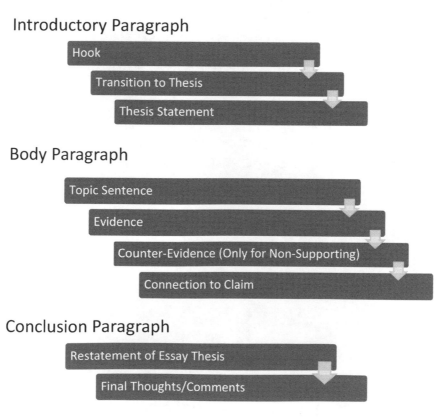

Hook

Transition to Thesis

Thesis Statement

Body Paragraph

Topic Sentence

Evidence

Counter-Evidence (Only for Non-Supporting)

Connection to Claim

Conclusion Paragraph

Restatement of Essay Thesis

Final Thoughts/Comments

Essay Planning Worksheet

Essay Prompt: _____
_____

Claim:

Three Reasons:

Thesis Statement:

Essay Outline:

Introduction

Body Paragraph 1

Body Paragraph 2

Body Paragraph 3

Conclusion

Essay Writing Worksheet Page 1

Introductory Paragraph

Hook: _____

_____

Transition to Thesis: _____

_____

Thesis Statement: _____

_____

Body Paragraph 1

Topic Sentence: _____

_____

Evidence/Counter-evidence: _____

_____

_____

Connect to Claim: _____

_____

Body Paragraph 2

Topic Sentence: _____

_____

Evidence/Counter-evidence: _____

_____

_____

Connect to Claim: _____

_____

Essay Writing Worksheet Page 2

Body Paragraph 3

Topic Sentence: _____
_____

Evidence/Counter-evidence: _____
_____
_____

Connect to Claim: _____
_____

Conclusion

Restate Thesis: _____
_____

Final Thoughts: _____
_____

Sample Essay: Original Version

The following sample essay is included with and without annotation. Use the unannotated version to practice identifying the components you have learned. Use the annotated version to check your answer.

How To Choose a Good Pet

Seventy percent of U.S. households, or about 90.5 million families, own a pet, according to the 2021-2022 National Pet Owners Survey conducted by the American Pet Products Association. Although each family is different, there are three key characteristics that should be considered when choosing a pet. These are compatibility with the owner's lifestyle, a good temperament, and the likely expenses.

Compatibility with the owner's lifestyle is the first factor to consider when choosing a pet. A pet that is a good match for the owner's living situation, and available time and resources will be more likely to thrive and be a happy and well-adjusted member of the household. For example, a high-energy breed may not be a good fit for an owner who works long hours and has limited time for exercise. A more laid-back breed may be a better choice in this situation. Additionally, it is important to consider any allergies or sensitivities that the owner or other household members may have, as certain pets may be more likely to trigger allergic reactions. Taking the time to choose a pet that is compatible with the owner's lifestyle and living situation can help to ensure that the pet is a good fit for the family.

The temperament of the animal is the next factor to consider when choosing a pet. For example, a pet that is calm and gentle may be a good choice for a family with young children, while a more energetic and playful pet may be better for an active owner. It is also important to consider the temperament of the pet in relation to its breed or species. For example, certain dog breeds may be more energetic or prone to barking, while certain cat breeds may be more independent or aloof. Understanding the temperament of a particular pet can help to ensure that it is a good fit for the owner.

Sample Essay: Original Version continued,

The third factor to consider when choosing a pet is the expenses involved. The costs of pet ownership can vary greatly depending on the type of pet and its specific needs. Some common expenses include food, veterinary care, supplies, training and grooming. Before choosing a pet, you should consider the typical costs for that breed and age of animal. A pet that is a good fit for your family will not cause any additional financial hardship.

In conclusion, pet ownership can be a rewarding and fulfilling experience, but before choosing a pet, you should consider your lifestyle, the animal's temperament and the likely expenses. If you consider these three factors when making a decision, you are sure to end up with a wonderful pet that works well for your family.

References

"Pet Industry Market Size, Trends & Ownership Statistics." 2022. American Pet Products Association.
https://www.americanpetproducts.org/press_industrytrends.asp

Sample Essay: Annotated Version

How To Choose a Good Pet

[**Hook**: Seventy percent of U.S. households, or about 90.5 million families, own a pet, according to the 2021-2022 National Pet Owners Survey conducted by the American Pet Products Association.] [**Transition to Thesis:** Although each family is different,] [**Thesis Statement**: there are three key characteristics that should be considered when choosing a pet. These are compatibility with the owner's lifestyle, a good temperament, and the likely expenses.]

[**Transition and Topic Sentence**: Compatibility with the owner's lifestyle is the first factor to consider when choosing a pet. A pet that is a good match for the owner's living situation, and available time and resources will be more likely to thrive and be a happy and well-adjusted member of the household.] [**Evidence/Support**: For example, a high-energy breed may not be a good fit for an owner who works long hours and has limited time for exercise. A more laid-back breed may be a better choice in this situation. Additionally, it is important to consider any allergies or sensitivities that the owner or other household members may have, as certain pets may be more likely to trigger allergic reactions.] [**Link Back to Claim**: Taking the time to choose a pet that is compatible with the owner's lifestyle and living situation can help to ensure that the pet is a good fit for the family.]

[**Transition and Topic Sentence**: The temperament of the animal is the next factor to consider when choosing a pet.] [**Evidence/Support**: For example, a pet that is calm and gentle may be a good choice for a family with young children, while a more energetic and playful pet may be better for an active owner. It is also important to consider the temperament of the pet in relation to its breed or species. For example, certain dog breeds may be more energetic or prone to barking, while certain cat breeds may be more independent or aloof.] [**Link Back to Claim**: Understanding the temperament of a particular pet can help to ensure that it is a good fit for the owner.]

Sample Essay: Annotated Version continued,

[**Transition and Topic Sentence**: The third factor to consider when choosing a pet is the expenses involved.] [**Evidence/Support**: The costs of pet ownership can vary greatly depending on the type of pet and its specific needs. Some common expenses include food, veterinary care, supplies, training and grooming. Before choosing a pet, you should consider the typical costs for that breed and age of animal.] [**Link Back to Claim**: A pet that is a good fit for your family will not cause any additional financial hardship.]

[**Transition and restate thesis**: In conclusion, pet ownership can be a rewarding and fulfilling experience, but before choosing a pet, you should consider your lifestyle, the animal's temperament and the likely expenses.][**Future Thought**: If you consider these three factors when making a decision, you are sure to end up with a wonderful pet that works well for your family.]

References

"Pet Industry Market Size, Trends & Ownership Statistics." 2022. American Pet Products Association.
https://www.americanpetproducts.org/press_industrytrends.asp

Part 5

Answer Key

In this section, you will find answer keys for the exercises in the workbook.

If your answers are different, that's okay. There are multiple possible answers for most of the exercises.

Answer Key: Pages 11, 12, 14

Essay Prompt	Topic Words	Direction Words
What is the biggest challenge facing today's students?	biggest challenge facing today's students	What is: means *explain with reasons*
What are the advantages and disadvantages of school uniforms?	school uniforms	What are the advantages and disadvantages.
Compare and contrast two different hobbies.	two different hobbies	Compare and contrast
Why is it a good idea to graduate high school?	good idea to graduating high school	Why: means *explain with reasons*
What makes a good pet?	good pets	What makes: means *what are the characteristics of* (a good pet)

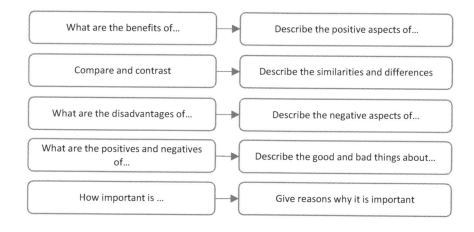

Essay Prompt	Which is a Strong Claim?
What is the biggest challenge facing today's parents?	• Dealing with screentime is the biggest challenge parents face.
Should zoos be banned?	• Zoos should not be banned.
What is the right age to get a phone?	• Children should get phones before they are teenagers.

Answer Key: Pages 15, 17

Essay Prompt	Possible Claims
What are the benefits of learning a musical instrument?	• Learning an instrument has many benefits. • Learning an instrument has more benefits than disadvantages.
What are the advantages and disadvantages of a school lunch program?	• School lunch programs have both advantages and disadvantages. • School lunch programs have more advantages than disadvantages. • School lunch programs have more disadvantages than advantages.
Compare and contrast two different sports.	• Basketball and soccer have both similarities and differences. • Basketball and soccer are more alike than different. • There are few similarities between basketball and soccer.
Why is it a good idea to study hard?	• Studying hard is a good idea for several reasons. • There are no good reasons to study hard.
What makes a good hobby?	• There are three main elements to a good hobby. • Good hobbies have four main features.
How important is kindness? Explain your answer.	• Kindness is the most important characteristic that humans can possess. • Kindness is not necessary. • Kindness is extremely important.

Claim	Reason	Relevant to Claim? Yes/No
Peanut butter sandwiches make the best lunch.	Peanuts butter sandwiches became popular during the 1920s.	No
The internet has changed our daily life.	We can now access information without going to the library.	Yes
The internet has changed our daily life.	The internet can be slow.	No
Climate change is a big problem.	Heat waves are increasing.	Yes
Climate change is a big problem.	Climate change is caused by fossil fuels.	No
Fresh fruit is the best dessert.	My favorite fruit is apples.	No
Fresh fruit is the best dessert.	Fruit contains many nutrients.	Yes
Schools should start at 7 am.	We would have lots of free time in the afternoon to do sports.	Yes
Schools should start at 7am.	I live close to my school.	No

Answer Key: Pages 18, 19, 21

Claim	Possible Reasons
Schools should have no more than ten students per class.	1. Students have more opportunity to participate. 2. The teacher can spend more time with each student. 3. Small classes get better results.
Teenagers should get paid for doing homework.	1. Teenagers would focus more in school if they knew money was involved. 2. Teenagers would do more homework to earn more money. 3. Teenagers will learn the feeling of reward for earning money.
You do not need a college degree to be successful.	1. You can start your own business without a college degree. 2. You can work your way up in some companies without a degree. 3. Many good careers, such as a trades careers, don't need a degree.

Claim	Possible Reasons
Schools should not assign homework.	*FOR:* *1.* Low-income families may not be able to afford supplies for homework or have a computer/internet connection. 2. Students should be encouraged to be active outside school hours, not sitting down more. *AGAINST:* 1. Homework teaches time management skills 2. Homework helps teachers see how well the students understand the material.
All teenagers should get a part-time job.	*FOR:* 1. Teaches responsibility. 2. Earn pocket money *AGAINST:* 1. Less time for homework 2. Teenagers should be active outside of school time. Many part-time jobs are not active.

Claim	Reasons	Thesis statement
Getting a part-time job is a good idea for teenagers.	1. Builds your resume 2. Gain work experience 3. Earn money	Getting a part-time job is a good idea for teenagers because it builds their resume, they can gain work experience and they can earn money.
The internet has changed our daily life.	1. No longer need printed maps, we can use GPS. 2. Can access information without going to the library. 3. Can connect with friends more easily.	The internet has changed our lives significantly. For example, we can use GPS instead of printed maps, access information without going to the library, and connect with friends more easily.
Cats and dogs are more similar than different.	SIMILARITIES 1. Both are able to survive in the wild. 2. Both have territorial instincts. DIFFERENCE 1. Dogs more social and cats more solitary.	Even though dogs and cats differ in their sociability, cats and dogs are more similar than different because they are both able to survive in the wild and both have territorial instincts.

Answer Key: Pages 22, 24, 25, 26

Thesis Statement	Problem	Possible Rewrite
Going to college is an excellent way to get a good job.	Claim but no reasons.	Going to college is an excellent way to get a good job because many jobs require degrees, these jobs usually pay more, college is a good place to network to find a good job.
This paper is about the internet and how bad it is.	Claim is vague and there are no reasons.	The internet is bad for children because there is inappropriate content, cyberbullies, and too much use can lead to low self-esteem.
Pollution is a big problem.	Claim is vague and there are no reasons.	Pollution is a big problem in America because it affects people's health, their access to clean drinking water and can also kill crops.
This paper is about good teachers. They are organized, helpful and inspiring.	Reasons without a clear claim.	Good teachers have three main characteristics: They are organized, helpful and inspiring.
School lunchtime should be longer because it's good for kids.	Only one reason and it is quite vague.	School lunch times should be longer because longer lunches leads to better student performance, increased physical health and increased social-emotional health.

Essay Prompt: What is your favorite movie? Explain why.	**Claim:** My favorite movie is 'Up'.
Reasons: 1. Cute characters 2. Exciting plot 3. Satisfying ending	**Thesis Statement:** My favorite movie is 'Up' because of its cute characters, exciting plot and satisfying ending.

Essay Prompt: Does class size matter?	**Claim:** Class size matters.
Reasons: 1. Affects student participation 2. Affects student learning 3. Affects sense of community.	**Thesis Statement:** Class size does matter because it affects students' participation, learning and sense of community.

Essay Prompt: What are the advantages and disadvantages of a college education?	**Claim:** A college education is a good idea.
Reasons: 1. Leads to better-paying careers 2. Leads to more satisfying careers 3. Can be expensive	**Thesis Statement:** Even though college is expensive, a college education is a good idea because it leads to more satisfying and better-paying careers.

Essay Prompt: What are the pros and cons of social media?	**Claim:** Social media is overall good.
Reasons: 1. promote civic responsibility and engagement 2. encourage diversity 3. But can lead to cyber bullying.	**Thesis Statement:** Even though social media can lead to cyberbullying, overall social media is a positive influence because it can promote civic responsibility and engagement, encourage diversity and help people build relationships.

Answer Key: Pages 28, 29

Thesis: School uniforms are a good choice because they are inexpensive, make it easier to get ready for school and promote a sense of community.

Introduction: School uniforms are a good choice because they are inexpensive, make it easier to get ready for school and promote a sense of community

Body Paragraph 1: Write about how school uniforms are inexpensive and why that means school uniforms are a good choice.

Body Paragraph 2: Write about how school uniforms make it easier to get ready for school and why that means school uniforms are a good choice.

Body Paragraph 3: Write about how school uniforms promote a sense of community and why that means school uniforms are a good choice.

Conclusion: Because school uniforms are inexpensive, make it easier to get ready for school and promote a sense of community, they are a good choice for any school.

Thesis: Homework should be banned because it takes too much time, cuts into family time and doesn't increase grades.

Introduction: Homework should be banned because it takes too much time, cuts into family time and doesn't increase grades.

Body Paragraph 1: Write about how homework takes too much time and why that means homework should be banned.

Body Paragraph 2: Write about how homework cuts into family time and why that means homework should be banned.

Body Paragraph 3: Write about how homework does not increase grades and why that means homework should be banned.

Conclusion: Because homework takes too much time, cuts into family time and doesn't increase grades, it should be banned in all schools.

Thesis: Even though smaller classes are expensive, smaller classes are better because students can get more help and form a closer bond with their fellow students.

Introduction: Even though smaller classes are expensive, smaller classes are better because students can get more help and form a closer bond with their fellow students.

Body Paragraph 1: Write about how students get more help in smaller classes and why that means classes should be smaller.

Body Paragraph 2: Write about how smaller classes leads to closer bonds and why that means classes should be smaller.

Body Paragraph 3: Write about how smaller classes are more expensive. Give reason why this is not a problem and so smaller classes are the best option.

Conclusion: Even though smaller classes are expensive, because students can get more help and form a closer bond with their fellow students, smaller classes are better.

Answer Key: Page 30

Thesis: **Students should not be allowed to bring phones to class because they distract the student from learning, distract other students and can also distract the teacher.**

> **Introduction** Students should not be allowed to bring phones to class because they distract the student from learning, distract other students and can also distract the teacher.

> > **Body Paragraph 1**: Write about how phones distract students from learning and why that means phones should be banned in class.

> > **Body Paragraph 2**: Write about how phones distract other students and why that means phones should be banned in class.

> > **Body Paragraph 3**: Write about how phones can distract the teacher and why that means phones should be banned in class.

> **Conclusion**: Because phones distract the student from learning, distract other students and can also distract the teacher, they should be banned in class.

Thesis: **Students should be allowed to bring phones to class because they can access information quickly, set reminders for homework and access educational apps.**

> **Introduction**: Students should be allowed to bring phones to class because they can access information quickly, set reminders for homework and access educational apps.

> > **Body Paragraph 1**: Write about how students can access information and why that means phones should be allowed in class.

> > **Body Paragraph 2**: Write about how students can set homework reminders and why that means phones should be allowed in class.

> > **Body Paragraph 3**: Write about how students can access educational apps and why this means phones should be allowed in class.

> **Conclusion**: Because students can access information quickly, set reminders for homework and access educational apps using their phones, phones should be allowed in class.

Answer Key: Pages 32, 33

Essay Prompt: Should students be allowed to wear makeup to school?

Claim: Students should be allowed to wear makeup to school.

Three Reasons:
1. It's a way of expressing yourself.   2. It helps with confidence.   3. Health reasons

Thesis statement: Students should be allowed to wear makeup to school because it is a way of expressing oneself, it can help with confidence, and some students may need to wear makeup for health reasons.

Outline:

Introduction: Students should be allowed to wear makeup to school because it is a way of expressing oneself, it can help with confidence, and some students may need to wear makeup for health reasons.

Body Paragraph 1: Explain how makeup allows you to express yourself and why this is a good thing.

Body Paragraph 2: Explain how makeup increases your confidence and why this means students should be allowed to wear makeup to school.

Body Paragraph 3: Explain why some students need to wear makeup for health reasons and why this means all students should be allowed to wear makeup.

Conclusion: Wearing makeup is a way of expressing oneself, it can help with confidence, and some students may need to wear makeup for health reasons. For these reasons, students should be allowed to wear makeup to school.

Essay Prompt: What are the pros and cons of using games to teach?

Claim: Using games to teach has both pros and cons.

Pros		Cons	
1. Increased engagement		1. Some topics too detailed for games	
2. Develop collaboration skills		2. Can be time-consuming	

Thesis statement: Teachers need to make their own decisions about when to use games to teach because while games can increase engagement and develop collaboration skills, games are not suitable for all topics and can be much more time-consuming than just teaching the content.

Outline:

Introduction: Teachers need to make their own decisions about when to use games to teach because while games can increase engagement and develop collaboration skills, games are not suitable for all topics and can be much more time-consuming than just teaching the content.

Body Paragraph 1: How games increase engagement and why that means teachers should use them.

Body Paragraph 2: Explain how games develop collaboration skills and why that means teachers should use them.

Body Paragraph 3: Explain how some topics are too complicated to teach with games and why that means teachers shouldn't use games.

Body Paragraph 4: Explain how games are more time consuming than direct teaching and why that means teachers should not use games.

Conclusion: While games can increase engagement and develop collaboration skills, games are not suitable for all topics and can be much more time-consuming than just teaching the content. For these reasons teachers need to make their own decisions about when it is appropriate to use games in their classrooms.

Answer Key: Pages 37, 40

1. Hook	[1 Sweet desserts have been around since the middle ages.]
2. Transition to Thesis	[2 These days there are many desserts to choose from. However,]
3. Thesis Statement	[3 ice-cream is the best dessert because it is delicious, easy-find and comes in many flavors.]

1. Hook	[1 There are more than 2 billion websites on the internet.]
2. Transition to Thesis	[2 While not all of these websites are good,]
3. Thesis Statement	[3 children should be allowed to access the internet because the internet is educational, fun, and there are many online games that families can play together.]

1. Hook	[1 Children often ask for internet access.]
2. Transition to Thesis	[2 However, not everything children want is good for them.]
3. Thesis Statement	[3 Children should not be allowed to access the internet because staring at a screen is unhealthy, there are dangerous places on the internet and their time is better spent playing with friends.]

1. Hook	[1 Only 20% of US schools start their day at 7:45 or earlier.]
2. Transition to Thesis	[2 Many school are wasting part of the day.]
3. Thesis Statement	[3 School should start at 7am because it allows plenty of time to play in the afternoon, time for an afternoon job and lots of time to do homework.]

Essay Topic	Potential Hooks
What are the advantages and disadvantages of school uniforms?	From the halls of private schools to the classrooms of public institutions, school uniforms have long been a controversial topic.
	School uniforms: a necessary evil or a source of school pride?
	Are school uniforms the answer to improving academic performance and reducing bullying, or do they stifle creativity and individuality?

Essay Topic	Potential Hooks
Why is it a good idea to graduate high school?	Graduating high school is an important milestone in a person's life and marks the transition from adolescence to adulthood.
	About 10 % of students don't graduate high school. Is this a good idea?
	What happens if you don't graduate high school?

Answer Key: Pages 42, 44, 45

Hook	October 14 is National Dessert Day.
Transition	While all delicious desserts should be celebrated,
Thesis Statement	Fresh fruit is the best dessert because it is nutritious, delicious and easy to prepare.

Hook	The first known use of the word 'dessert' was in the 1600s.
Transition	While dessert fashions have changed over the years, these days
Thesis Statement	Fresh fruit is the best dessert because it is nutritious, delicious and easy to prepare.

Hook	The US National School Lunch program costs more than 13 billion dollars per year.
Transition	Despite this huge cost,
Thesis Statement	Schools should include a free lunch because it helps students learn, helps poorer students and reduces childhood obesity.

Essay Topic: Should students be allowed to bring phones to class?

Hook: In today's digital age, phones have become an integral part of our daily lives, and the question of whether students should be allowed to bring them to class is a controversial one.
Transition: Although students are strongly attached to their phones,
Thesis Statement: Students should not be allowed to bring phones to class because they distract the student from learning, distract other students and can also distract the teacher.

Essay Topic: Should students be allowed to bring phones to class?

Hook: Over 95% of teenagers own a smart phone.
Transition: Given their expertise in using these devices,
Thesis Statement: Students should be allowed to bring phones to class because they can access information quickly, set reminders for homework and access educational apps.

Essay Topic: Should teens be allowed to drink coffee?

Hook: Coffee is a widely consumed beverage that is enjoyed by people of all ages.
Transition: Given how popular it is,
Thesis Statement: Teens should be allowed to drink coffee because caffeine can lower a person's risk for heart disease, increase alertness and focus, and coffee contains some healthy antioxidants.

Essay Topic: Should teens be allowed to drink coffee?

Hook: About 31% of teens in the US drink coffee daily.
Transition: Despite its popularity,
Thesis Statement: Teens should not be allowed to drink coffee because caffeine can cause the body to lose calcium, can bring on a jittery feeling, and can cause insomnia.

Answer Key: Pages 48, 50, 51

1. Topic Sentence	[1 Caffeine can lower your risk of heart disease.]
2. Evidence/Support	[2 According to researchers from the University of Colorado, a cup of coffee can lower your risk of heart disease by 5%.]
3. Connection to Essay Claim	[3 Teenagers should be allowed to drink coffee so they can lower their risk of heart disease.]

Topic Sentence	[1 Children should be allowed to access the internet because it is very educational.]
Evidence/Support	[2 You can find videos that explain school subjects such as English or science. You can play online games to practice math.]
Connection to Essay Claim	[3 Children need internet access to benefit from these educational resources.]

Essay Thesis: Children should be allowed to access the internet because the internet is educational, fun, and there are many online games families can play together.	
Claim: Children should be allowed to access the internet.	Reason # 3: there are many online games families can play together.
Possible Topic Sentence: Another benefit of accessing the internet is that there are many online games that families can play together, providing a fun and engaging way to spend time together.	

Essay Thesis: Students should be allowed to bring phones to class because they can access information quickly, set reminders for homework and access educational apps.	
Claim: Students should be allowed to bring phones to class.	Reason # 3: Students can access educational apps.
Possible Topic Sentence: Another benefit of bringing phones to class is that students can access a variety of educational apps that offer a range of learning opportunities and resources, including interactive games, tutorials, and virtual classrooms.	

Essay Thesis: Teens should be allowed to drink coffee because caffeine can lower a person's risk for heart disease, increase alertness and focus, and coffee contains some healthy antioxidants.	
Claim: Teens should be allowed to drink coffee.	Reason # 2: Caffeine can increase increase alertness and focus.
Possible Topic Sentence: Another benefit of drinking coffee is that caffeine can increase alertness and focus.	

Answer Key: Pages 53, 54

Topic Sentence: Learning a second language benefits your brain.

Evidence Brainstorm/Research:
1. Learning a second language can improve executive function skills.
2. Learning a second language improves memory.

https://bmcgeriatr.biomedcentral.com/articles/10.1186/s12877-021-02051-x
https://www.whitbyschool.org/passionforlearning/learning-a-new-language-helps-brain-development

---

Evidence Sentence(s):

Studies have shown that learning a second language can improve executive function, which is the cognitive process responsible for controlling and coordinating other cognitive skills. Executive function skills include planning, problem-solving, and decision-making, and are important for a range of activities, including learning and academic performance. Learning a second language can also improve memory and attention, as it requires the brain to process and retain new information. Research has shown that bilingual individuals tend to have better memory skills than those who only speak one language.

Topic Sentence: Caffeine can have health benefits.

Evidence Brainstorm/Research:
1. Moderate caffeine intake can lower the risk of heart attacks
2. Caffeine has been shown to improve insulin sensitivity, which can lower the risk of developing type 2 diabetes.

https://www.medicalnewstoday.com/articles/how-does-caffeine-reduce-heart-disease-risk
https://www.mayoclinic.org/diseases-conditions/type-2-diabetes/expert-answers/blood-sugar/faq-20057941

Evidence Sentence(s):

Some studies have shown that moderate caffeine intake can lower the risk of heart attack and stroke. In addition, caffeine has been shown to improve insulin sensitivity, which can lower the risk of developing type 2 diabetes.

Topic Sentence: Smoking is bad for your health.

Evidence Brainstorm/Research:
1. Smoking causes heart disease.
2. Smoking causes cancer.

https://www.cdc.gov/tobacco/data_statistics/fact_sheets/fast_facts/index.htm
https://www.who.int/news-room/fact-sheets/detail/cancer

Evidence Sentence(s):

Smoking is a major cause of cardiovascular disease, including heart attack, stroke, and peripheral artery disease. According to the Centers for Disease Control and Prevention (CDC), smoking is responsible for about 1 in 3 deaths from cardiovascular disease in the United States. Smoking is also a major cause of cancer, particularly lung cancer, but it can also increase the risk of other types of cancer, such as bladder, kidney, and pancreatic cancer. The World Health Organization (WHO) estimates that about one-third of all cancer deaths are caused by tobacco use.

Answer Key: Pages 56, 58

Essay Claim: Schools should have uniforms.
Topic Sentence: School uniforms instill a sense of equality.
Evidence Sentences: When students wear a school uniform, competitive feelings about looks are reduced. Students can stand out because of their character and not their clothes.
Connection to Claim Sentence: Because of the importance of equality for students, schools should have mandatory school uniforms.

Essay Claim: Public transit should be free.
Topic Sentence: Free public transport would reduce the number of cars on the road.
Evidence Sentences: Global warming is a serious issue and if public transport was free, more people would use it, reducing the need for cars. One train could take 2000 cars off the road.
Connection to Claim Sentence: Reducing car use would directly benefit the planet's climate. This is another strong reason why public transit should be free.

1. Topic Sentence	[1 Coffee does have some negative affects.] [2 Specifically, caffeine can cause insomnia because it is a stimulant.]
2. Evidence/Support	[3 However, this problem is easily avoided by only drinking coffee before 3pm.] [4 Therefore, the potential for insomnia should not prevent teens from drinking coffee.]
3. Counter-evidence	
4. Connection to Essay Claim	

1. Topic Sentence	[1 The internet has many dangerous places.] [2. The news often contains articles about some of the problem areas and dangers.]
2. Evidence/Support	[3 However, the real world has dangers, too. Rather than banning children from the internet, we should be teaching them how to be safe in all the worlds they inhabit.]
3. Counter-evidence	[4 The dangers of the internet are no reason to ban children from the internet.]
4. Connection to Essay Claim	

Answer Key: Pages 61, 64

Essay Claim: Schools should have uniforms.
Topic Sentence in non-supporting paragraph: Buying school uniforms is an added expense for families.
Evidence supporting topic sentence: School uniforms can cost about $200 per outfit. And families still have to buy everyday clothes as well.
Counter-evidence sentence: However, the need for everyday clothes is much less when a uniform is worn five days per week. Hence overall, less money will be needed for clothes.

Essay Claim: Public transit should be free.
Topic Sentence in non-supporting paragraph: Providing free transit would be extremely expensive.
Evidence supporting topic sentence: The city would need to buy more buses and pay more drivers.
Counter-evidence sentence: However, the city is also likely to save with less road congestion, which diminishes the need for expensive infrastructure like new highways and wider bridges.

There are over 100 buildings in the world more than one thousand feet tall. <u>However</u>, the tallest building is the Burj Khalifa. The Burj Khalifa is amazing for several reasons.

<u>First</u>, this building is 2,722 feet tall, almost 1 kilometer! Can you imagine how tall that is?

<u>Second</u>, the Burj Khalifa cost $1.5 billion dollars to build. Construction of the Burj Khalifa started in 2004 and finished in 2009.

The Burj Khalifa building is in Dubai. <u>Although</u> most people think Dubai is a country, it is not. <u>In fact</u>, it is one of the seven Emirates in the United Arab Emirates.

Even the name of the building is interesting. Burj means tower in Arabic. Khalifa is the name of the leader of the United Arab Emirates.

The Burj Khalifa has won many awards. It has broken records for the highest restaurant and the highest swimming pool. <u>In addition</u>, it has the highest observation deck in the world.

<u>To sum up</u>, the Burj Khalifa is truly amazing!

Answer Key: Pages 65, 66, 67, 69

Because the weather was bad, Jenny took an umbrella with

In conclusion , these are the reasons why we should have a longer lunch break.

Tamra likes art. _However_ , her favorite subject is math.

I cleaned the kitchen, did my homework and tidied my room. _As a result_ , I should be allowed to go play with my friends.

For example: The right amount of screen time can vary greatly depending on an individual's age, needs, and interests. For example, the World Health Organization suggests limiting screen time to no more than one hour per day for children under the age of five.

In addition: In addition, it is important to recognize that excessive screen time can have negative impacts on physical and mental health.

To begin with: Changing screen time habits can be difficult. To begin with, it may be helpful to set limits on screen time, schedule regular breaks from screens, and find alternative activities to engage in when not using screens.

In conclusion: In conclusion, all users should consider how much time they spend on screens.

However: However, other viewpoints exist.

Next: Next, let's consider the opposite viewpoint.

Similarly: Similarly, data from schools also supports this viewpoint.

Although: Although, this might seem like a problem, recent data shows that it is less common than previously thought.

Frequently: Frequently, the weather is suggested as a cause of these problems.

Thesis Statement: Students should not be allowed to bring phones to class because they distract the student from learning, distract other students and can also distract the teacher.

Reason I choose to write about: phones distract students from learning

Topic Sentence: The most important reason why phones should be banned in class is because they distract students from learning.

Evidence brainstorming/research:
1. students using phone in class had lower grades.
https://www.hendrix.edu/uploadedFiles/Academics/Faculty_Resources/2016_FFC/Cell%20phone%20use%20during%20class%20and%20grades.pdf

Evidence Sentences:
A recent research study found that students who used their phones for non-academic purposes during class had lower grades than those who did not

Link to Essay Claim: This is clear evidence that having phones in class is detrimental. Hence, students should not be allowed to bring phones to class.

Answer Key: Pages 70, 72, 74

Thesis Statement: Although teenagers think smoking is cool, smoking should be banned because it is addictive, bad for your health and costs a lot.

Reason I choose to write about: Smoking costs a lot

Topic Sentence: One of the simplest arguments against smoking is that it costs a lot.
Research/Brainstorming:
1. Financial cost as well as health cost.
https://chronicdata.cdc.gov/Policy/Map-of-Average-Cost-Per-Pack-of-Cigarettes-Orzecho/t2jw-y7rh + other links

Evidence Sentences: According to data from the Centers for Disease Control and Prevention (CDC), the average cost of a pack of cigarettes in the United States in 2020 was $6.92. This means that if you smoke one pack of cigarettes per day, it will cost you around $250 per month or $3,000 per year. In addition to the cost of cigarettes, smoking can also incur other costs, such as the cost of health care for smoking-related illnesses and the cost of lost productivity due to absenteeism and decreased work performance. Overall, the cost of smoking can be significant and can have a major impact on a person's financial well-being.

Link to Essay Claim: These large costs are another reason why cigarette smoking should be banned.

Original Thesis	Reworded Thesis
Students should not be allowed to bring phones to class because they distract the student from learning, distract other students and can also distract the teacher.	In conclusion, because phones distract the student from learning, distract other students and can also distract the teacher, students should not be allowed to bring phones to class.
Fresh fruit is the best dessert because it is nutritious, delicious and easy to prepare.	To sum up, fruit is nutritious, delicious and easy to prepare. For this reason, fresh fruit is the best dessert.

Essay Thesis: Teens should be allowed to drink coffee because caffeine can lower a person's risk for heart disease, increase alertness and focus, and coffee contains some healthy antioxidants.

Final Thoughts: Teens have many restrictions on their lives. Their coffee consumption need not be one of them.

Essay Thesis: Students should learn a second language in school because it increases their employment potential, benefits their brain, and gives students an understanding of other cultures.

Final Thoughts: What are your thoughts? Will you choose to learn a second language?

Essay Thesis: Although there are many delicious desserts, fresh fruit is the best dessert because it is nutritious, delicious and easy to prepare.

Final Thoughts: Given all the benefits, I hope you will try it!

Answer Key: Pages 77, 79, 80

Essay Prompt	Possible Titles
Should students be allowed to use phones in class?	• Student Phones in Class • Student Phones in Class: Okay or Not? • Why Student Phones should be Banned
What is the best breakfast?	• The Best Breakfast: A Definite Answer • What is the the Best Breakfast? • There is No Best Breakfast
Should zoos be banned?	• Zoos: Should They be Banned? • Zoos: An Argument for Banning Them • Why Zoos Should Not Be Banned
What challenges do today's teenagers face that are different from the challenges their parents faced?	• Teenage Challenges • Teenagers Today: The Challenges They Face • The Different Challenges Faced by Today's Teenagers
Compare and contrast two novels set in your state or city.	• The Similarities and Differences of Two Local Novels • A Comparison of Two Local Novels • How Two Local Novels See This State Differently.

Congratulations on finishing the workbook!

You now know everything you need to know to write strong 5-paragraph essays. Have fun being an essay expert!

Why not check out the other books in the Step-by-Step Study Skills series. Available in print & Kindle on Amazon.

And, don't forget to download the free editing checklist!

https://www.HappyFrogLearning.com/product/editingchecklist

Good luck with your essay writing and editing.

CERTIFICATE
OF
ACHIEVEMENT

THIS CERTIFICATE IS AWARDED TO

_____

IN RECOGNITION OF

_____

_____   _____

DATE   SIGNATURE

_____

TITLE